Whistle *Around* The World

by L.E. McCullough

FIFTY TUNES FOR PENNYWHISTLE OR FLUTE
FROM ALL OVER THE WORLD!

Standard notation with chord symbols

INCLUDES CD

Project editor and recording engineer: Peter Pickow

Order No. OK 65032
International Standard Book Number: 0.8256.0342.0

Exclusive Distributors:
Music Sales Corporation
257 Park Avenue South, New York, NY 10010 USA
Music Sales Limited
8/9 Frith Street, London W1D 3JB England
Music Sales Pty. Limited
120 Rothschild Street, Rosebery, Sydney, NSW 2018, Australia

Printed in the United States of America by
Vicks Lithograph and Printing Corporation

Oak Publications
a Part of the Music Sales Group
New York/London/Paris/Sydney/Copenhagen/Berlin/Tokyo/Madrid

Contents and Track Listing

Foreword

> "When Krishna plays the flute the whole world is filled with love. Rivers stop, stones are illumined, lotus flowers tremble; gazelles, cows, and birds are entranced; demons and ascetics enchanted."
>
> —from the *Bhagavata-Purana*, tenth century India

How long have people been trying to make sounds by blowing air over, into, and through a tube? We might never truly know the answer, but scientists have dated the six complete bone flutes discovered in 1999 at a Neolithic grave site in Jiahu, China, as being made—and played—nine thousand years ago. Created from the bones of the red-crowned crane, these flutes have five, six, and eight holes and are still playable.

And in Slovenia, near the town of Nova Gorica, a 1997 excavation of a Neanderthal campsite turned up flute fragments believed to date from around 50,000 B.C.E., give or take a few millennia. The material used to make this flute came from the femur of a young bear, which suggests that flute-playing in the Neanderthal period was not for the weak-of-heart.

Today, every country on the planet has some kind of whistle or flute in its traditional music legacy. Whistles and flutes encompass an enormous variety of sizes, shapes, fingerings, and materials, but there are some basic categories:

• **End-blown flute.** A flute in which the player's breath is directed against the sharp edge of the open upper end; also called **notched flute**, **vertical flute,** or **rim-blown flute.** *Nay, shakuhachi,* and *kaval* are examples.

• **Duct flute.** A flute that directs the player's air stream into a narrow duct. Duct flutes often have beaked mouthpieces, and some versions have no fingerholes, such as the *slidewhistle.* Also called **block flute.**

• **Fipple flute.** A type of duct flute sounded by a *fipple* and a *flue.* The *fipple* is the block in the mouthpiece that constricts the air to produce sound; the *flue* is the channel through which the air flows. A hole is cut in the wall of the flute below the fipple, the sharp edge known as the *lip.* The player's breath is directed by the flue against the lip. *Flageolets, tinwhistles,* and *recorders* are common examples. Also called **whistle flute.**

• **Nose flute.** A flute blown with air from the nose instead of the mouth. Nose flutes are chiefly used for ritual and healing purposes, since nasal breath is believed to contain the soul.

• **Vessel flute.** Flutes and whistles that have a globular (instead of tubular) shape and are often made in the shapes of human beings or animals. The *sweet potato* and *ocarina* are modern examples, *ocarina* meaning "little goose" in Italian.

• **Aeolian pipe.** A pipe sounded naturally by the wind; it may be stationary, attached to a tree or building, or mobile, such as the *kite flutes* of Asia that fly in the sky while making music.

Whistles and flutes have been in our language for several centuries. The word *whistle* is from the Old English *hwistle,* a ninth-century word meaning "pipe, flute, or whistle" and is related to the Old Norse *hvisla* ("whisper"), the Danish *hvisle* ("hiss"), and the Latin *fistula* ("pipe"). The word *flute* entered the English language in the fourteenth century, deriving from *flaüte* (Old French) and *flaut* (Old Provence), words that may well have come from the Latin *flaujol,* derived from *flatus* ("blowing, blast, breathing").

This book visits forty-five countries with more than two hundred types of whistles and flutes. We hope you will enjoy the selection and extend your exploration into this fascinating world of musical air.

Australia
The Wallaby Track

The first European settlers of Australia were mainly from the British Isles. Though they brought their own tinwhistles, flutes, and recorders, they quickly became enamored of a native Aboriginal instrument called the *didgeridoo*—an end-blown flute between four and five feet long made from wood or bamboo that gives a low, resonant, vibrating sound. The player blows straight into the *didgeridoo,* which often has a beeswax mouthpiece or rim covered with tree gum resin. The *didgeridoo* was traditionally used for ceremonial tribal rites but is now played around the world. "On the wallaby track" is a "strine" expression (Australian slang) that refers to a "swagman" (laborer) going from ranch to ranch in search of work. This traditional song is believed to have evolved from a poem written in the 1860s by Australian poet E. J. Overbury who celebrated life in "the bush."

Roll up your bun - dle and make a neat swag, Col - lar on - to your bil - ly can and the old tuck - er bag. It's no dis - grace to be seen with your swag on your back, While search - ing for work on the wal - la - by track.

Bosnia
Kolo

The peoples of Bosnia, Croatia, Slovenia, Slavonia, Macedonia, and Serbia have an astonishing diversity of whistle and flute instruments, many of them originally brought by the Turks who ruled the Balkan region for several centuries. These include: *kaval, sviralja* (end-blown flutes); *duduk, frula, jedina, churlika* (whistle flutes); and *svardonica,* a whistle flute with two parallel pipes in a single block of wood. Most have cylindrical bores and five to seven fingerholes. *Kolo* is a type of round dance popular throughout the Balkans, especially Serbia, Croatia, and Bosnia. The word *kolo* means "wheel" in Croatian, and there are hundreds of different *kolo* dances accompanied by melodies like this one from Bosnia.

Brazil
Zing-za

Pife is a cylindrical end-blown flute of Brazil between ten and twenty-five inches long and made of wood or cane. It has two and a half octaves, five or six fingerholes and is often played with the *zabumba* (a friction drum) in an ensemble called *cabaçal.* "Zing-za" is a rural *samba,* a dance from which many of the dances seen in Brazil's world-famous Carnaval celebration derive.

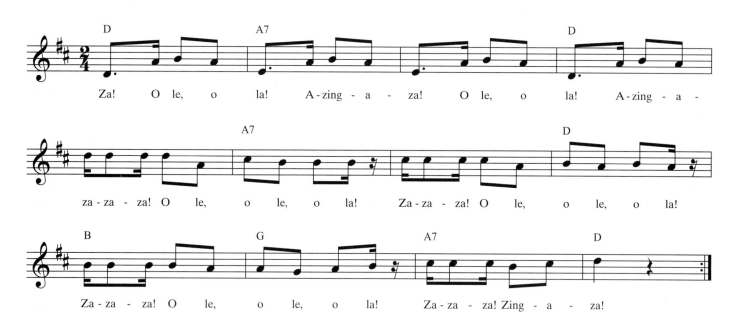

Za! O le, o la! A - zing - a - za! O le, o la! A - zing - a -

za za za - za! O le, o le, o la! Za - za - za! O le, o le, o la!

Za - za - za! O le, o le, o la! Za - za - za! Zing - a - za!

Brittany
Kimiad ar Soudard Yaouank

Brittany is a region of northwest France with a vigorous tradition of music derived from its ancient Celtic heritage. Breton wind instruments include *biniou koz* ("old bagpipe"), *biniou bihan* ("little bagpipe"), the one-drone bagpipe *veuze,* the double-reed *bombarde,* and a clarinet called *treujeun gaol* ("cabbage stump"). "Kimiad ar Soudard Yaouank" is a *gwerz,* a Breton ballad based on a historic or legendary event. This nineteenth-century song by the poet Prosper Proux recounts the feelings of a young Breton soldier leaving his home to fight in a foreign war.

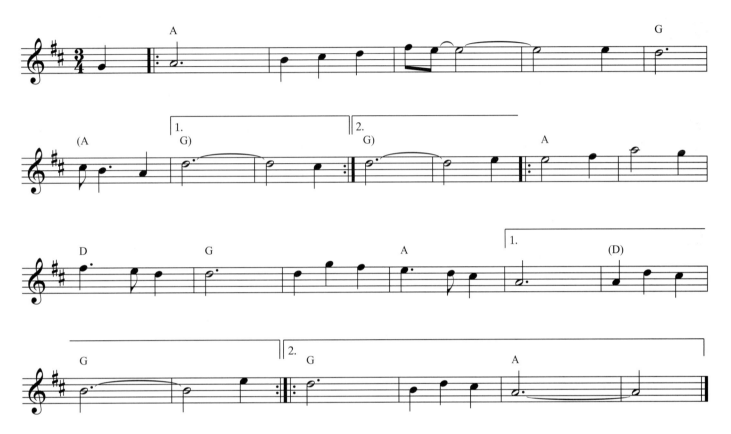

Bulgaria
Elenke

In addition to *duduk* and *kaval,* a popular wind instrument played in Bulgaria is the
svirchitsa, a conical whistle flute about twelve inches long with six fingerholes that is a
smaller version of the Bosnian *svirka.* In past times, these instruments were favored
by shepherds, who played melodies to sentimental love songs like "Elenke"
in order to entertain themselves and their flocks.

Canada
Sur la rivière

The first European settlers to Canada in the 1500s brought flageolets, pipes, and recorders, but there is evidence suggesting earlier inhabitants also played flutes and whistles of a more primitive sort. A burial site in southern Labrador dating to 7500 B.C.E. contained a well-used bone flute, possibly used in tribal rituals. Signaling whistles imitating animal sounds were also common among the native peoples, as was a willow-bark duct flute similar to the *seljefløyte* of Norway. The popular Quebec song "Sur la rivière" is from the vast repertoire of lumber-camp songs that flourished in Canada during the 1800s when the lumber industry was at its height.

Canada
The Greenland Man's Tune

This tune is a blend of Inuit and European traditions, a relic from the days when hundreds of whaling ships shuttled back and forth across the Atlantic from Canada to Britain and Northern Europe. Inuit music often incorporated the sounds made by birds and animals, sometimes using overtones to sound two or more notes at the same time. Some of these melodies recall the unique throat-singing style *(katadjak')* popular among Native Canadian people, where two singers faced each other and traded short rhythmic motifs in an effort to keep the song going without pause.

China
Song of the Four Seasons

The *hsiao* (sometimes spelled *xiao*) is a notched end-blown flute with five fingerholes and one thumbhole that has been played in China since the twelfth century B.C.E. It is made of bamboo and is approximately twenty-seven inches in length. The *hsiao* is related to the Korean *thung so*. The transverse flute commonly found in China today is *di zi* (pronounced *dee-ch*), also made of bamboo and equipped with six fingerholes. Membranes are placed over the embouchure hole and top fingerhole to give the *di zi* a reedy timbre. Other Chinese winds include *hsiian* (porcelain globular flute), *shao erh* (clay whistle), and *hua mei chiao tse* (bamboo bird whistle). "Song of the Four Seasons" is a popular song believed to have come from the Daur people of western China.

Congo
Pauline Mineure

Small end-blown whistles are popular among several peoples living in the Congo: *mbamba nsia* (Bembe), *mbmabi* (Kikongo), *mbana* (Mangbetu), and *nsiba* (Bembe). The instruments are made from gazelle or antelope horn and are seven to eight inches long. "Pauline Mineure" is a tune in the *soukous* style, a genre created by Congo musicians in the 1950s influenced by records of Cuban *rhumba* music and Antilles *zouk*.

Cuba
La Guaracha

Much traditional Cuban music is played on a five-key wooden transverse flute typically made from redwood or ebony. This flute is called the *charanga flute* because it is played in the Cuban *charanga* orchestra that also uses piano, strings, vocals, and percussion. The *guaracha* is a style of Cuban dance music with roots in eighteenth-century satirical street songs. This tune is an imitation of roosters fighting and was performed in costumes suggesting feathers and birdlike dance steps.

Dominican Republic
La Gozadera

"La Gozadera" is a melody in the *merengue* style, a type of dance music that came to the Dominican Republic in the early 1800s from neighboring Haiti. It is thought to be derived from the *mouringue* music of the Bara, a Bantu people of Madagascar. In addition to wooden flutes, traditional *merengue* bands used string and percussion instruments. In the *gaga* style of Dominican ritual music popular in the countryside, musicians play long bamboo tubes with leather mouthpieces fixed over one end, a sort of Caribbean *didgeridoo*. The term *gozadera* signifies a happy-go-lucky attitude and has recently become a form of Venezuelan pop music.

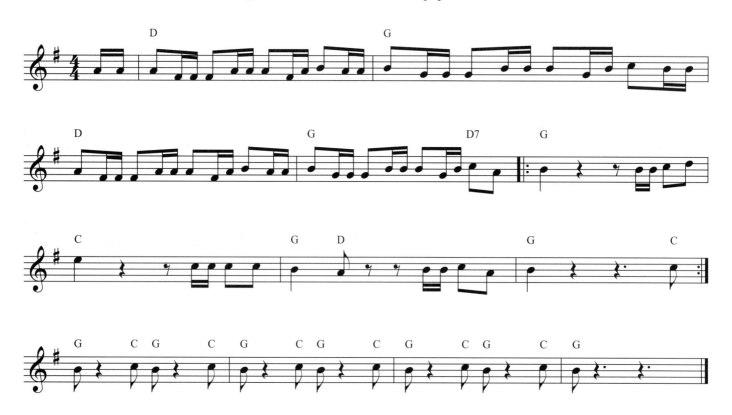

England
The Flying Cloud

The *pipe and tabor* was a popular instrument in medieval England and is seen in many woodcuts and artworks of the period. The pipe was a three-hole, keyless cylindrical flageolet about twelve inches long played in combination with a small snare drum, or *tabor,* slung over the player's neck. Using the left hand to hold the pipe, the player used the right hand to beat the tabor and keep rhythm to the melody. With two front fingerholes and a rear thumbhole and the use of overblown notes called *harmonics,* the pipe player could attain a range of an octave and a half. *Whittle and dubb* is another name for the pipe and tabor combination, and it is said that these musicians entertained crowds at plays during Shakespeare's day. In 1803 woodwind maker William Bainbridge of London created an "English flageolet" pitched in D with six holes at the front, one at the back, and a sponge chamber to absorb moisture from the player's breath. "The Flying Cloud" is an eighteenth-century ballad that tells the lamentable tale of a young sailor forced into piracy and then hanged for his nautical crimes.

France
Le Petit Homme

France is home to many varieties of flutes and whistles, including the *sifflet a roulette* (tinwhistle), *galoubet* (pipe and tabor), *larigot* (medieval whistle made from a sheep's thigh bone), and *flageolet*—the end-blown whistle flute that reached Europe from Asia in the eleventh century and is a precursor to the modern piccolo. By the seventeenth century, the flageolet typically had six fingerholes, four on the front and two on the back for the player's thumbs, and was of conical shape with a two-octave range. In the eighteenth century it was used to teach canaries to sing and also appeared in compositions by Handel, Gluck, and Mozart. By the nineteenth century, the French flageolet was an elaborate instrument with as many as six keys. "Le Petit Homme" is a song in bourrée rhythm that comes from the Massif Central region of France and tells the story of a henpecked husband.

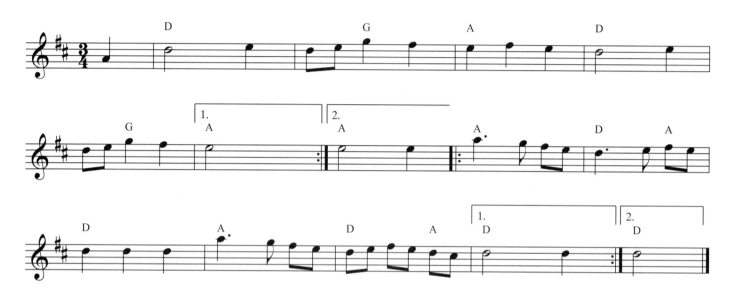

Germany
Das Wandern ist des Müllers Lust

Germany has been a breeding ground for whistles and flutes since before the Crusades. In medieval times, the *schwegel* (from the German word for "shinbone") was a pipe and tabor–like instrument popular among the peasantry. The *narrenflöte* (also called *jester's flute*) was a whistle flute with a globular center. The German Renaissance composer and musicologist Praetorius made note of the *dulceflöte,* which combined a transverse flute body and a whistle head. "Das wandern ist des Müllers Lust" ("To Wander Is the Miller's Joy") is a song on the delights of being a wandering miller and dates from the early nineteenth century with words by Wilhelm Müller and music by Carl Friedrich Zöllner.

Greece
Garifalia

Two wind instruments that epitomize the music and mythology of the ancient Mediterranean are the *aulos* (double pipes) and *syrinx* (panpipes) of Greece. In modern Greece, the *suravli* is an end-blown flute made of cane, wood, or bone with six fingerholes and a rear thumbhole, which is also known by the names *phlogera, dzamara,* and *phlanton.* "Garifalia," or "Carnation," is a popular Greek love song; it was featured in the 2002 World's Largest Concert that saw over eight million children from around the world perform the same songs at the same hour.

Hungary
Három Pohár

"Három Pohár" ("Three Glasses") is a Gypsy dance song. Many of the flutes and whistles found in Hungary originated in rural areas and are associated with shepherds. *Furulya* is a shepherd's pipe found in many lengths and tunings, typically one to two feet in length with six or seven fingerholes and a range of an octave; a smaller version is called *pikula*. *Hosszu furulya* is a long five-hole shepherd's pipe about three feet long. *Tilinko* is a cylindrical wooden whistle about two feet long; it has no fingerholes, and different notes are obtained by opening and closing the bottom end with the fingers. *Czakan* is a musical walking stick; it has six front fingerholes, one rear thumbhole, and two small holes in the knob serving as blowholes.

India
Pinnal Kolattam

Two fipple flutes found throughout India are *bansuri* and *venu,* both made of cane or bamboo. *Bansuri* is between two and twenty inches long with four to seven fingerholes; *venu* is about four feet long and has eight fingerholes. "Pinnal Kolattam" ("Weaving Dance") is a melody accompanying a famous dance from Tamilnadu, performed around a pole using ribbons and sticks that weave the ribbons into plaits. According to legend, there once lived an *asura* (violent semi-god) who terrorized the people. Some girls went to the *asura* and danced Pinnal Kolattam, so pleasing the *asura* that he surrendered all his evil designs and let the people live in peace.

Indonesia
Man Paman Goejang Djarang

Suling is the generic name for several types of bamboo flutes and whistles found throughout Indonesia, especially in Java, Bali, and Sunda: *suling idong* (nose flute), *suling kechil* (ring flute), *suling nyawa* (whistle flute), *suling reog* (end-blown flute), and *suling degung* and *suling gede* used in *gamelan* ensembles. *Sundari* is an Indonesian *Aeolian pipe,* a type of wind instrument sounded by the wind. Aeolian pipes made of bamboo are popular across Southeast Asia and are often attached to kites; when flown aloft, these pipes send music over long distances. "Man Paman Goejang Djarang" is a children's song sung during the telling of fairy tales, or *dongèng.*

Iran
Daramad

Nay is an end-blown flute found throughout the Middle East from Iran to Egypt; in North Africa it is called *qasaba.* Made of cane, *nay* and *qasaba* have five to six fingerholes and one rear thumbhole for overblowing. The player holds the instrument at a slant and blows across the edge of the mouth hole producing a rich, breathy sound. *Nay* and *qasaba* are usually about two feet in length and are made in different pitches. "Daramad" is a prelude or melodic introduction that sets the mood of the mode, the *dastgah,* from which a longer instrumental piece will be created.

Ireland
Haste to the Wedding

Pennywhistle, Tin Flute, Feadóg Stáin—you will hear all those names to describe the *tinwhistle*, a fipple flute with six fingerholes first manufactured in its current form in 1843 by Robert Clarke of England. Clarke's tinwhistles were inspired by wooden whistles that had begun to appear in the British Isles earlier in the century; he made his whistles out of tin with a wooden mouthpiece block inserted into the top of the conical tube of approximately twelve inches. In the 1950s other tinwhistles, notably Generation, were produced that used a separate plastic mouthpiece and a cylindrical tube. By the early 1900s the tinwhistle had become a staple instrument in traditional Irish music, and there are currently scores of tinwhistle makers around the world. "Haste to the Wedding" is a double jig, one of the most plentiful tune types in the Irish dance repertoire.

Israel
Zemer Lach

Klezmer is the dance music created by Jewish musicians in Eastern Europe during the eighteenth and nineteenth centuries. With influences from Russian, Romanian, Polish, German, Ukrainian, and Turkish folk music along with elements drawn from cantorial singing and Hassidic chants, *klezmer* has come to symbolize the vibrant spirit of Ashkenazic Jewish culture. While traditional *klezmer* music featured the clarinet, modern *klezmer* ensembles have included flute, recorder, saxophone, oboe, even tinwhistle. "Zemer Lach" is played to accompany the *hora,* a popular chain-circle dance from the Balkans.

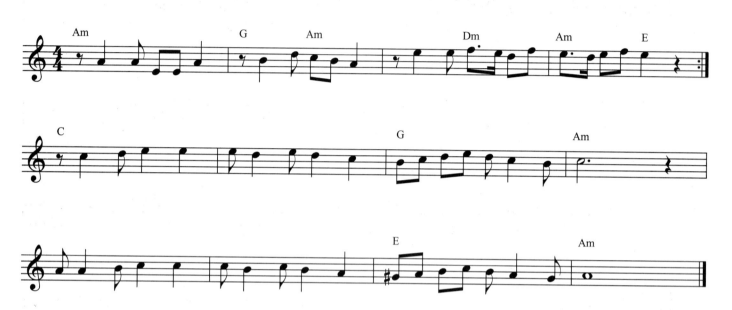

Italy
L'Avvelenato

Italy has several unique wind instruments, including *launeddas* (triple pipe) of Sardinia, *friscalettu* (cane flute) of Sicily, and *firlinfeu* (panpipes) of Brianza. "L'Avvelenato" ("The Poisoned Lover") is a variant of "Lord Randal," the British ballad known throughout Europe from Iceland to Hungary. In this version, a man hunting in a sacred wood is poisoned by a fairy disguised as his true love.

Japan
Fishing Song from Haragama

Shakuhachi is an end-blown flute made from bamboo, about twenty-one to twenty-two inches long, with four fingerholes and one rear thumbhole. The embouchure has a small notch, and by changing the angle of this hole, subtle changes in pitch and timbre can be produced. Introduced from China in the tenth century, *shakuhachi* is used as a solo instrument in Japanese classical and folk music and was traditionally played by wandering Buddhist priests. *Hitoyogiri* and *tempuku* are thinner, shorter versions with a wooden upper rim that appeared in Japan in the 1500s. "Fishing Song from Haragama" is a song from Fukushima district in northeast Japan.

Mexico
El Tecolote

Whistles and flutes in Mexico and Central America date back three thousand years and have been made of clay, cane, stone, bamboo, bone, metal, and wood. Some are pottery pieces made in the shape of animals, gods, or flowers: ocarinas *(huilacatixtli, nexhuiliztli),* simple clay whistles *(chilitli, cohuilotl),* or end-blown whistle flutes with three to seven fingerholes *(cocoloctli, tlapitzalzintli).* Small flutes six to eight inches in length with two, three, and four tubes that could produce melodies with chords, such as the triple flute of Tenenexpan, Veracruz, also existed. European influence is evident in the *tambor y flauta* (drum and flute) combination heard in rural regions like Sinloa, Chiapas, and Oaxaca.
"El Tecolote" ("The Owl") is a *huapango,* a genre of dance tunes in §§ from southeastern Mexico.

Native American: Navaho
Rainbow Cradle Song

In traditional Native American society, flutes were used by young men for courting. Found throughout North America, these "love flutes" (or *siyo tanka* in Lakota) were short fipple or duct flutes made of whatever natural materials were handy—bamboo, hollow reeds, bone, or wood—and occasionally decorated with animal images. Each player composed his own melodies that served as signals that might say to his beloved, "Meet me by the willow grove." Some *siyo tanka* have been found that reached an octave in range. Modern Native American flutes are made from hardwoods and come in a variety of scales and sizes, typically with five or six fingerholes.

Hush, my lit - tle white shell in your rain - bow cra - dle;

Do not cry, my white shell, do not cry, my white shell;

Go to sleep my white shell, go to sleep my white shell.

Native American: Yuchi
Lonesome Flute

Many Native American legends feature the mythical flute player, Kokopelli. Rock drawings of Kokopelli's distinctive hump-backed, flute-playing image are found throughout North America. He was said to be a wandering minstrel from Mexico whose music had many magical powers. Tribes in the arid American Southwest believed that Kokopelli's flute carried messages to the gods requesting rain for crops, and Kokopelli was also thought to be able to give babies to families without children simply by throwing out seeds he carried in his knapsack. This Yuchi melody from the Southeastern U.S. was recorded in 1900 by a man named Jim Tiger.

Netherlands
Te Kieldrecht

The *gemshorn* ("goat's horn" in German) is a fipple flute about twelve to fourteen inches long, with three to six fingerholes, rear thumbhole, and sharply tapering conical bore that gives it an octave range. Popular among European musicians during the sixteenth and seventeenth centuries, it was made from the horn of an ox or a chamois (a small antelope) and produced a soft, plaintive sound originally used by shepherds to calm their flocks. "Te Kieldrecht" is a satirical song about the lazy girls of Kieldrecht in the region of Flanders.

New Zealand
Waiata Aroha

The Maori people of New Zealand have several whistles and flutes in their musical culture made from wood, bone, and stone. *Koauau* is an eight-inch, conical-bore, end-blown flute made of wood or bone. It has three fingerholes and is blown at an angle and sometimes played as a nose flute. *Porutu* is similar to *koauau* but about twice as long. Originally made from the tooth of a whale, *nguru* is a curved flute and only three or four inches long with two to four fingerholes. *Putorino* is an end-blown flute some eighteen inches long with one large fingerhole in the center carved to resemble the human mouth. If blown at the wider end, it gives a deeper, "male" voice; if blown across the central hole in the top of the instrument, it produces a softer, "female" voice. *Whio* is a six-inch whistle flute with four fingerholes, made from albatross bone and used by men as a courting flute. "Waiata Aroha" is a melody from a class of love songs composed by women.

Nigeria
Olurombi

Nigerian wind instruments include *aji-an igede* (tinwhistle), *dunda* (pointed flute associated with children), and *opikeh* (side-blown talking instrument made from antelope horn once used to give signals in battle). *Oja* is a "talking" three-hole wooden whistle from eastern Nigeria often used with *ekwe, udu,* and *igba* drums. An *oja* player is said to make the instrument sound several words while leading dances or announcing visitors. "Olurombi" is a song from the Yoruba tribe that tells the legend of a woman Olurombi who asked the gods to make her rich in exchange for the sacrifice of her first-born daughter.

Panama
Un Tamborito

Kammu is an end-blown flute of the Cuna and Ashlushlay people of Panama. Made of a bamboo tube about twenty-eight inches long, *kammu* has two fingerholes and is often played with one hand while the performer uses the other hand to shake the *nasis,* a gourd rattle filled with seeds. The *tamborito* is the national dance of Panama; dancers move in a circle and clap hands and stamp feet as they sing, imitating the rhythm of the *tamboro* drum that accompanies them.

Peru
Achachau

Quena is an end-blown flute found throughout the Andean Highlands. Made from bone, metal, clay, cane, gourd, and, nowadays, even plastic, *quena* is a cylindrical tube with six front fingerholes, one rear thumbhole, and a notched or beveled groove at the top for the mouthpiece. *Quena* comes in various lengths from twelve to twenty-four inches (from *quenilla* to *quenacho*); the typical standard model of today is tuned to G major. Other native Andean winds include *serere* (small wooden whistle), *suxca* (globular flute made of deer or guanaco skull), and *pincullu*, a cylindrical bamboo whistle flute between twelve and twenty inches long with two front fingerholes and one rear thumbhole. Though *zampoña* is a Spanish word, this panpipe was played in the Andes more than fifteen hundred years ago. Also called *siku, antara, toyo,* or *rondador, zampoña* typically consists of one set of six tubes and one set of seven tubes bound together, each tube of a different pitch to form a complete scale. Played individually and in groups, *zampoña* is blown across the top of the tube. "Achachau" ("It's Hot!") is a *huayno* from the South Highlands of Peru.

Poland
Podkóweczki Dajcie Ognia

Whistles and flutes of Poland include *fujarka,* a whistle flute with six to eight fingerholes, and
piscolka and *fujarka wielkopostna,* small pipes without fingerholes that are overblown to produce
harmonics. In mountain regions long wooden flutes between four and seven feet long such as *rog
pastierski* and *trabita* are used by shepherds to signal their flocks. "Podkóweczki Dajcie Ognia"
("Click Your Heels") is a *mazurka,* a dance performed by four or eight couples.

Portugal
Cançao a Lua

Flauta pastoril is a three-hole whistle and *pífano* a six-hole fife that have been played in Portugal since the Middle Ages. *Flauta pastoril* is typically accompanied by *tamboril* (a tabor drum); *pífano* is often heard in consort with *caixa* (snare drum) and *bombo* (bass drum). "Cançao a Lua" ("Song to the Moon") is a *modinha,* a style of romantic love song.

Puerto Rico
Mataron a Elena

The flute is a featured instrument in several Puerto Rican folk music ensembles, particularly those that perform *plena,* a satirical song-and-dance form developed in the early 1900s. A *plena* is a "periodico cantado"—a kind of living newspaper that mixes current events with gallows humor. The vocal and instrumental breaks in a *plena* are performed in a call-and-response pattern that suggests a live street setting. This *plena,* from the repertoire of 1930s bandleader Manuel A. Jiménez, "El Canario," is "Mataron a Elena" ("They Killed Elena") and mimics women gossiping about a neighbor:

They cut up Elena, they cut up Elena,
And they took her to the hospital.
Don't be afraid, dear one, I've come to tell you
They cut up Elena, mama, I'll never forget her!

Romania
Shpilt-Zhe Mir Dem Nayem Sher

Romania shares flutes and whistles with several of its neighbors, including *frula* from Serbia, *kaval* from Bulgaria, and the double-flute *dvojnice* from Croatia. Native to Romania are *tilinca*, a cylindrical end-blown flute without fingerholes, and *fluiere*, a six-hole wooden pipe. "Shpilt-Zhe Mir Dem Nayem Sher" is a song that extols the popularity of the *sher*, an East European dance similar to the American square-dance.

Play that lovely tune for me
The sher that they're all dancing.
I'm in love with a handsome lad
But I dare not go romancing.

Russia
Down along the Mother Volga

Russian winds include three types of whistle flute (*svirel, dudka, sipovka*) along with *sopilka* (end-blown flute), *kurai* (conical flute), *svistulka* (clay whistle), *kuvichki* (whistling wooden pipe), and *podvaynaya svirel,* a double whistle with the longer whistle pitched a fourth lower than the shorter. "Down along the Mother Volga" is a popular Russian folk song from the 1800s believed to have been composed by Ivan Osipov, a highwayman known as Vanka Kain.

Scotland
Farewell Tae Kemper

Whistle playing in Scotland goes back to at least the fourteenth century, the estimated creation date of the bronze, six-hole Tusculum whistle discovered in North Berwick in 1907. Shepherds and street buskers alike played whistles throughout the country using flageolet-like instruments made of clay, wood, and reeds. From the mid 1800s Scottish whistle players took up the Clarke tinwhistle, and the instrument became a staple of Scottish "bothy bands," folk music ensembles that flourished in rural Scotland during the late nineteenth to early twentieth centuries.

"Farewell Tae Kemper" is a traditional Scottish march.

South Africa
Ngoma Kurila

Whistles and flutes abound in the Southern part of Africa, including the Sotho people's *lekolilo,* the *mokoreie* of the Bangwaketse, the *nanga ya ntsa* from Vendaland, the *umtshingo* found among the Zulu and Pondo. The best-known South African whistle tradition is *kwela* music, a mix of traditional South African styles with American blues and jazz music. Developed in Soweto during the 1940s and 1950s, *kwela* (derived from Zulu and Xhosa *ikhwelo,* "whistling, a shrill whistle") was performed on six-hole metal Hohner and Generation tinwhistles by master players such as Elias Lerole, Willard Cele, Lemmy Special, and Spokes Mashiyane. "Ngoma Kurila" is a drum-dance song.

Spain
Muiñiera d'a Fonte

Spanish flutes and whistles include *flaviol* from Catalonia and the Pyrenees Mountains, a small ivory flageolet with three front fingerholes, two rear holes, and three closed keys; in Castille, it is called *flautilla*. In Galicia, the whistle flute *pito* is popular, with three front fingerholes and two rear holes. Among the Basque people, *txistu* is a three-hole whistle flute tuned in F and made of ebony or box-wood. It is usually accompanied by a small snare drum called *tanborín* played by the same musician. *Txistu* also appears as *silbote* (a larger size tuned in B♭, B, or C) and *txirula* (smaller and tuned in C an octave above *silbote*); *txirula* is accompanied by *ttun-ttun,* a six-string zither played as if it were a stringed drum to give bass and harmony to the melody. "Muiñiera d'a Fonte" ("The Fountain Muiñiera") is a tune from Galicia.

Sweden
Nu Är Det Jul Igen

The eight-hole *Spilåpipa* ("chanter") and six-hole *Härjedalspipa* ("Pipe of Härjedalen") are two wooden whistle flutes found throughout Sweden and neighboring Norway. *Sälgflöjt* ("willow flute") is a whistle with no holes, traditionally made from willow bark; a natural harmonic scale is obtained by opening and closing the end hole, thus altering air pressure. "Nu Är Det Jul Igen" ("Christmas Is Here Again") is a popular Swedish Yuletide song with the lyrics:

Christmas is here again,
Christmas is here again,
And Christmas goes right on till Easter.
Then Easter's here again,
Then Easter's here again,
And Easter goes right on till Christmas.

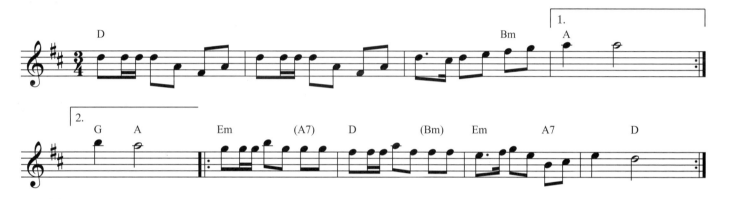

Syria
Al Ya Zane

A very old instrument known throughout the Arabic music world since the Middle Ages, *shabbaba* is the end-blown cane flute of Syria (*shabbai* among the Druse of Israel). About a foot in length, it has six front fingerholes and a rear thumbhole and is played today largely in rural areas. "Al Ya Zane" ("O, You, Zane") is a love song.

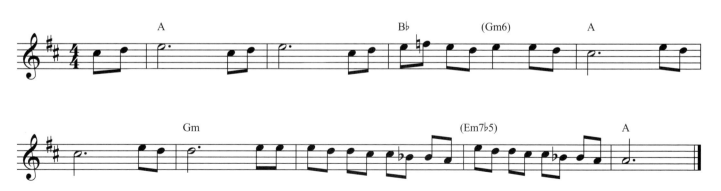

Thailand
Ngam Sang Duan

Khlui is a fourteen-hole end-blown flute with seven front fingerholes, two front thumbholes, one membrane hole covered by tissue paper, and four vent holes at the lower end. Made of wood, ivory, or bamboo, *khlui* are cylindrical and come in three sizes, ranging from fourteen to twenty-four inches in length. They are played vertically and resemble the Japanese *shakuhachi* in sound and playing technique. "Ngam Sang Duan" is a tune played to accompany the popular Rum Wong dance of Central Thailand.

Trinidad
Tingalayo

On 2 August 1498, Christopher Columbus first anchored off the island of Trinidad and ordered his sailors to dance and play pipe-and-tabor music for the native inhabitants, the Arawak. The natives, however, took this display as a war challenge and sent a shower of arrows at the ship! Had the Arawak responded musically, they would have used wind instruments called *guamo* and *cobo* made from conch shells. In the ensuing centuries, Trinidad has become a melting pot of African, Asian, and European musical traditions, including calypso and steel drum music. "Tingalayo" is a children's song popular throughout the West Indies.

Tingalayo, run my little donkey run
Tingalayo, run my little donkey run

Me donkey walk, me donkey talk
Me donkey eat with a knife and fork
Me donkey eat, me donkey sleep
Don't get too close to his hind feet

Turkey
Oyun Havasi

Turkey is home to several members of the end-blown flute family, notably *nay, supurga,* and *qawal* along with the whistle flute *duduk,* found throughout the Balkans. The Turkish *duduk* is between nine and sixteen inches long and has a cylindrical bore with a flared mouthpiece; it has six finger-holes, and the player typically hums a drone while playing melody. "Oyun Havasi" ("Dance Song") is played frequently at weddings.

Uganda
Bwalobera Nkere

Endere (also called *nyamulere)* is a notched flute of the Ganda tribe. It may be made of bamboo, wood, or reed and has four fingerholes. *Endere* come in five sizes and are played in ensembles of harp, xylophone, and drums that were formerly part of the king's royal court. "Bwalobera Nkere" ("The Frogs") is a mourning song for a member of the tribe.

United States
Hua-hua'i

Two types of whistle instruments come from Hawaii, both nose-blown. *Ohe-hano-ihu* is made of bamboo and is about an inch in diameter, six to eighteen inches long, the blowhole at the top end. With the left hand, the player holds the end of the pipe squarely against the lip so the right nostril slightly overlaps the edge of the embouchure. An *ohe-hano-ihu* typically has five tones and two octaves: F and G in the lower register, F, G, and A in the octave above. *Pu-á* is a round, ocarina-like whistle made from a gourd the size of a lemon and pierced with two or three finger holes. Like the *ohe-hano-ihu*, the *pu-á* is found throughout Polynesia. This tune, "Hua-hua'i" ("Outburst"), is a love song from the nineteenth century.

United States
Dennis McGee's Two-Step

This tune is from Cajun fiddler Dennis McGee (1893–1989). McGee grew up near Eunice, Louisiana, and began recording commercially in 1929 for Vocalion Records with accordionist Amédé Ardoin and fiddlers Sady Courville and Ernest Frugé. Having learned from his father and grandfather, his performing style gives an idea of what Cajun music might have sounded like early in the nineteenth century; several of his tunes suggest the presence of Irish and Scots influences mixed with the French.

United States
The Girl I Left behind Me

Fifes and whistles have been used since the Middle Ages for the purpose of signaling commands in drill and battle. In the American Revolution, military music was considered so important to the Colonial army that George Washington appointed a special inspector to oversee that every unit had properly trained musicians. "The Girl I Left behind Me" was brought to America from the British Isles during the 1600s and popularized as a fife-and-drum tune for the Continental Army during the American Revolution. Irish painter, novelist, and songwriter Samuel Lover (1797–1868) added these lyrics:

I'm lonesome since I crossed the hill,
And o'er the moor and valley,
Such heavy thoughts my heart do fill,
Since parting with my Sally.
I'll seek no more the fine and gay,
For each but does remind me,
How swift the hours did pass away,
With the girl I left behind me.

Oh, ne'er shall I forget the night,
The stars were bright above me,
And gently lent their silv'ry light
When first she vowed she loved me.
But now I'm bound for Brighton camp,
Kind Heav'n may favour find me,
And send me safely back again,
To the girl I left behind me.

United States
Where Shall I Be?

Cane fife ensembles abounded in the Southern U.S. until the twentieth century, when they retreated to the deep woods of rural Georgia and Mississippi. These fifes, made from bamboo cane with five or six fingerholes, were accompanied by snare and bass drums found in bands like the Rising Star Fife and Drum Band led by Otha Turner (1909–2003) of Senatobia, Mississippi. They performed a repertoire with direct links to West Africa, predating other African-American idioms such as blues and jazz. "Where Shall I Be?" is a gospel tune from the 1930s composed by Andre Thomas. The words to the chorus are:

Where shall I be when that first trumpet sounds?
Where shall I be when it sounds so loud?
It will sound so loud, it will wake up all the dead.
Where shall I be when it sounds?

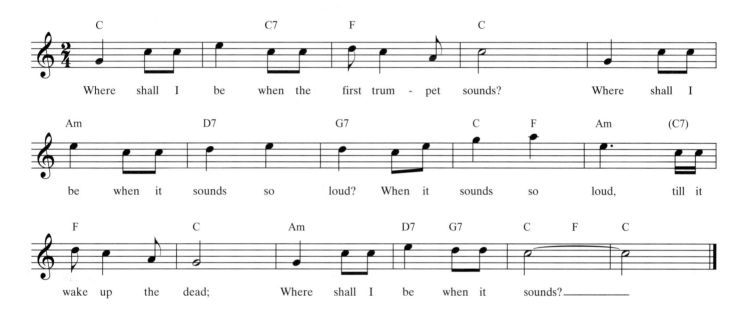

Wales
The Sweet Primroses

Wales shares the tradition of flutes and flageolets found in the rest of Britain. It also has its own unique wind instrument called the *pibgorn*, or *hornpipe*, the name used by thirteenth-century English writer Geoffrey Chaucer when mentioning it in his Canterbury Tales. The *pibgorn* is a pipe about twenty inches long with a curved cow-horn shaped bell and may be made of wood, bone, or horn. A single split-cane reed provides the sound, and there are six fingerholes and one rear thumbhole. Believed to be descended from shepherd's pipes played in ancient Asia, today's *pibgorn* plays an octave range starting on D above middle C. "The Sweet Primroses" is a broadside ballad first published in William Barrett's *English Folk Songs* (1909).

As I was walking one midsummer morning,
A-viewing the meadows and to take the air,
'Twas down by the banks of the sweet prim-e-roses,
When I beheld a most lovely Fair.

With three long steps I stepp'd up to her,
Not knowing her as she pass'd me by;
I stepp'd up to her, thinking to view her,
She appear'd to me like some virgin bride.

I said: Pretty maid, how far are you going?
And what's the occasion of all your grief?
I'll make you as happy as any lady,
If you will grant me one small relief.

Stand off, stand off, you are deceitful;
You are deceitful, young man, 'tis plain—
'Tis you that have cause my poor heart to wander,
To give me comfort 'tis all in vain;

I'll take thee down to some lonesome valley,
Where no man nor mortal shall ever me tell;
Where the pretty little small birds do change their voices
And ev'ry moment their notes do swell.

Come all you young men that go a-courting,
Pray give attention to what I say,
There's many a dark and cloudy morning
Turns out to be a sunshiny day.